CW00959499

Three Days of Rain

RICHARD GREENBERG

Three Days of Rain

Grove Press
New York

Published simultaneously in Canada
Printed in the United States of America

FIRST EDITION

Library of Congress Cataloging-in-Publication Data pending

Greenberg, Richard, 1958–
Three days of rain / Richard Greenberg
p. cm.
ISBN-10: 0-8021-4280-X
ISBN-13: 978-0-8021-4280-1
1. Architects—Drama.   2. Manhattan (New York, N.Y.)—Drama.   I. Title.
PS3557.R3789T48 2006
812'.54—dc22   2006041218

Grove Press
an imprint of Grove/Atlantic, Inc.
841 Broadway
New York, NY 10003

Distributed by Publishers Group West

www.groveatlantic.com

06 07 08 09 10   10 9 8 7 6 5 4 3 2 1

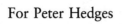

For Peter Hedges

Three Days of Rain was commissioned and originally produced by South Coast Repertory and was produced by Manhattan Theatre Club (Lynne Meadow, Artistic Director; Barry Grove, Executive Director) in New York City, on October 21, 1997. It was directed by Evan Yionoulis; the set design was by Chris Barreca; the costume design was by Candice Cain; and the light design was by Donald Hold; the sound design was by Red Ramona; the original music was by Mike Yionoulis; the special effects were by Gregory Meeh; and the production stage manager was Roy Harris. The cast was as follows:

Walker/Ned John Slattery

Nan/Lina Patricia Clarkson

Pip/Theo Bradley Whitford

Note: Lina rhymes with Carolina

Three Days of Rain will have its Broadway revival premiering on April 19, 2006, at the Bernard B. Jacobs Theatre in New York City, and is produced by Marc Platt and David Stone. It is directed by Joe Mantello; the scenic and costume design are by Santo Loquasto; the lighting design is by Paul Gallo; and the sound design is by David Van Teigham. The cast of the revival is as follows:

Walker/Ned Paul Rudd

Nan/Lina Julia Roberts

Pip/Theo Bradley Cooper

Setting

Act One

An unoccupied loft space in downtown Manhattan. 1995.

Act Two

The same space, only tenanted and happier. 1960.

Act One

1995

Setting: a somewhat dilapidated, spartanly furnished apartment located on a winding street in downtown Manhattan. Also a portion of that street.

Middle of the night.

Lights are dim.

A low hum of traffic. Walker is lying on the bed, eyes closed, listening. A car alarm sounds, abruptly shuts off. Walker opens his eyes.

Walker Meanwhile, back in the city. . . . Two nights of insomnia. In this room, in the dark . . . listening . . . soaking up the Stravinsky of it. . . . No end to the sounds in a city. . . . Something happens somewhere, makes a noise, the noise travels, charts the distance: The Story of a Moment.

God, I need to sleep! (*He lets out a breath, takes in the room.*)

Yes. All right. Begin. (*Lights fill in. Walker addresses us.*)

My name is Walker Janeway. I'm the son of Edmund Janeway, whose slightly premature death caused such a stir last year, I'm told.

As you're probably aware, my father, along with that tribe of acolytes who continue to people the firm of Wexler Janeway, designed all—yes, *all*—of the most famous buildings of the last thirty years. You've seen their pictures, you may have even visited a few. That Reform Synagogue in Idaho. The new library in Bruges. The crafts museum in Austin, that hospice I forget where, and a vertical mall in Rhode Island that in square footage actually exceeds the *state* of Rhode Island.

Years and years and years ago, with his late partner, Theodore Wexler, my father also designed three or four buildings that truly *are* distinguished, chief among them: Janeway House.

I know you know that one.

Everyone's seen that one picture, *LIFE Magazine*, April of '63, I think, where it looks lunar, I mean, like something carved from the moon, mirage-y—you remember that photo? It's beautiful, isn't it? It won some kind of non-Pulitzer Prize that year. People have sometimes declined my invitation to see the real place for fear of ruining the experience of the photograph.

Well. The real place, as it happens, is a private home out in the desirable part of Long Island. My grandparents commissioned it of my father, using all the money they had in the world, because, I guess, they loved him so much. Apparently, there was something there for a parent to love. Hard to imagine how they could tell, though, since he seldom actually spoke. Maybe he was lovable in a Chaplinesque way. Whatever, their faith paid off. The house is now deemed, by those who matter, to be one of the great private residences of the last half-century.

It's empty now.

My sister and I will inherit it today.

We'll be the only family present. Unless you count our friend, Pip, who is my late father's late partner's torpid son.

My mother would be with us, too, of course, but she's, um, like, well, she's sort of like Zelda Fitzgerald's less stable sister, so she can't be there. She's elsewhere, she's . . .

So, then, this is the story as I know it so far:

My father was more-or-less silent; my mother was more-or-less mad. They married because by 1960 they had reached a certain age and they were the last ones left in the room.

And then they had my sister who is somehow *entirely* sane.

And then they had me.

And my father became spectacularly successful, and his partner died shockingly young, and my mother grew increasingly mad, and my sister and I were there so we had to grow up.

And today we receive our legacy. (*Lights. Nan just arriving.*) You're here!

Nan Yes—

Walker How are you? You look great.

Nan Thank you.

Walker What a relief.

Nan (*Taking the place in.*) Is this where you're *living*?

Walker I had this image of—I was so afraid you were going to look like one of those women, you know, with a wedge cut who are forever eating oriental chicken salads in mall restaurants and going to musicals, but you *don't,* thank God!

Nan You were supposed to meet me.

Walker I—what?

Nan You said you'd—the *plan* was you'd meet me at the airport—

Walker Did we say that?—

Nan I took a cab, finally, when I realized waiting was a lost cause—

Walker I'm—what an idiot!

Nan Yes.

Walker I'm sorry.

Nan Well. You look thin.

Walker Oh, no—

Nan Ectomorph—*plas*mic, almost—are you eating?

Walker Oh God, I'm a *maw,* carbo-loading like a long-distance—well, actually, no, not in the last three days, *two* days—I tried to get a hamburger before but it didn't work out.

Nan I don't know what that means.

Walker I went into this restaurant, sat myself down, and asked for a bacon-cheeseburger, please—I was just so exactly like people, you would have—but then, the waiter? He said: "Thank you. And if you need anything, my name is Craig." So I said: "And if I *don't* need anything, what will your name be?" And he gave me this . . . really annihilating—I had to leave. *I thought I'd said it to myself! I* think maybe I'm not a people person anymore. I've missed you so much.

Nan Aren't we running late?

Walker Not at all—

Nan Will Pip be meeting us here or at—

Walker He's meeting us at Lawyer Fisher's—we have plenty of time, sit down, take off your coat, stay a while—(*She doesn't.*) Oh, Nan! I saw Pip on his *show!* Have you seen his—

Nan No.

Walker It was the first day I was back—

Nan And what day was that?

Walker I passed this store, there was this bank of television sets, all tuned to *Pip*—I went in—I insisted they turn up the volume—it was extraordinary. He plays someone named *Butte* who never wears a shirt and is carnally entangled with someone named *Savannah*—they must have met during an earthquake—anyway, he's all sort of rough and tender and monosyllabic and you'd never guess his father was a dead legend—

Nan Well, don't torture him about it.

Walker I . . . don't—

Nan Listen. Look. We'd better allow plenty of time for traffic—

Walker The appointment's not for—

Nan If you get snarled up in—

Walker It's three minutes by *rick*shaw, we won't—

Nan You come late for these estate lawyers and they penalize you in acreage—

Walker Oh God, I haven't seen you in a year and all you can talk about is itinerary—would you please please please just for a second drop this goddamned suburban alacrity and *hug* me? (*He hugs her. She barely submits. Then holds him tight. Then moves out of it.*)

Nan And just for the record: I do not live in the suburbs—I live in the city.

Walker (*Appalled.*) You live in *Boston.*

Nan Boston is a city.

Walker Boston is not a city, Boston is a *parish*.

Nan Oh, please.

Walker What could ever possibly happen to you on a street in Boston? You might, what, run into a *cleric* and *repent* something? Boston is only a city if you're a swan boat. You're supposed to realize that.

Nan Yes, I know: Boston is not a city, Detroit is not a city, Chicago is merely the exception that proves the rule about the Midwest—

Walker All that is true.

9

Nan I don't hold by any of it anymore, you know.

Walker (*Oddly serious.*) I sincerely hope that's not true. . . . Your life has made you so—

Nan You haven't even asked me one thing about my life since I—

Walker Yes. You're absolutely right. I'm sorry. How are you? How's Harry? How are the twins? They must be . . . different shapes, by now.

Nan . . . Nick has started to read.

Walker That's great.

Nan And Milly is ice skating like a—

Walker (*Overlaps.*) Oh, terrific.

Nan They're really spectacular.
     They're not twins, of course, but that's the sort of detail I don't expect you to have memorized.

Walker I know that, I—oh, look all children to me are, you know me and—they're all more or less one child taken to some unfathomable power, one *überkind,* all noisy and candid and tormenting, why don't you *sit?*

Nan *I don't* want *to sit!* (*Pause.*)

Walker . . . Nan?

Nan I thought you were dead this time.

Walker I, yes, you—

Nan I was certain of it, this time—

Walker I'm—

Nan There were things to think of at the funeral other than your absence, Walker. Did you ever consider us for a moment in this last year? Do you have any idea what it was like?

Harry hired detectives. It cost us a fortune. We learned *nothing*. For such a fuck-up you're incredibly gifted at getting lost. *Where were you?*

Walker Italy. (*Beat.*)

Nan Italy?

Walker Yes.

Nan Just . . . Italy?

Walker Yes, I know, anything short of Jupiter must sound prosaic after all you've been through, but—one town in particular for most of it. Well, eventually. In Tuscany.

Nan God!

Walker Um, I know, it's the most obvious possible pla—those detectives must have been quite second-rate; anyway, well, I'd been told nobody goes there anymore—an enormous lie, by the way—so I decided to try it out.

Oh, I had this memory—I think it was from a movie—of a field of bachelor's buttons and tall trees. I rented this very cheap but quite fine villa for a while—to study it, you know. I wanted to learn the bones of the building, I thought maybe I'd end up writing something. I spent months pretending I was that sort of person made ecstatic by olive oil, do you know? I very nearly *was,* for a bit. But nothing came of any of it.

Nan You just . . . walked out of your apartment; you abandoned—

Walker It had become—the filth of it—the chaos of it—it just happened. So I left. And *I did* go to the cemetery. The morning after the . . . event. Three o'clock or something.

Nan Jesus.

Walker It's nice where Ned is, isn't it? Under that tree, right by the water. He has a belvedere. I just sort of showed up

with my rucksack. I'd brought—oh God, you're not hearing this from me—I'd brought a candle. I'd decided to have a private ceremony. Luckily, it was raining, the candle, the wick wouldn't light. So I just sat on that big boulder by his grave, getting wet and chatting away like a moron. The dead man said nothing. So like the living.
Then, away.
Now here. Home to you.

Nan I could strangle you with my bare hands.

Walker Okay. . . .
Were they nice? The festivities, I mean?

Nan They were . . . big.

Walker (*Laughs a little.*) Yes.

Nan Very big.

Walker A *do*! And I missed it.

Nan It was filled with personages. The Finnish ambassador. Did he build something in Finland? The lieutenant governor—Kitty Carlisle!

Walker Hart.

Nan I forget sometimes . . . what he was, the scope of the life he'd made. The whole city turned out—

Walker And "mother"—was she—?

Nan No.
I wasn't permitted to tell her for, I think, two months. She didn't know he was dead for two months.
Or that you were missing.
Or her *name* half the time, probab—finally, they thought they'd found the right cocktail of drugs, it seems they'd brought her to equilibrium. I went there. Lina seemed fine. Truly. She was funny about her "recovery." She said: "Look

at me—all this nonsense because of jumbled hormones—and when I was young we thought it was an excess of *soul*."
Really: more Tallulah than ever. It's hard to connect that with Sanity Regained, but. . . . So I told her.

Walker And did she—

Nan Relapsed a couple of days later.
You haven't spoken to her in, what, five years?

Walker Three, *two*—

Nan You ought to. On a good day, she's exactly like you, only old.
. . . You're not planning on disappearing again any time soon, are you?

Walker Not planning it.

Nan Thank you.
But you're not living *here*. What *is* this place anyway? How did you find it?

Walker It was theirs.

Nan "Theirs." Whose?

Walker Ned's and Theo's. (*Beat.*)

Nan What do you—when?

Walker 1960. Right at the beginning.
I came back to town. All I had were my coat and a bag and about a billion traveler's checks—

Nan When did you have time to get traveler's—

Walker Most of my money is *in* traveler's checks. Anyway, I wandered around for a while. I stayed one night at this Catholic hotel on Twenty-Third Street, then—I forget. Then I remembered Lawyer Fisher. He told me about this. He gave me the keys. They lived here thirty-five years ago. They

13

were roommates, did you know that? That's the only thing I could find resembling a mattress. Do you suppose they were—

Nan Walker—God—

Walker It's possible—

Nan Not everyone is as sexually fluent as you, Walker—our loss, perhaps, but the *case*—he *kept* this?

Walker All this time. Intact, as far as I can make out. It was a rental at the start. He purchased it at some point, the whole building, I suppose it's ours now—oh! I found a picture from early on—that gallery across the street—(*Crosses to window.*)

Nan It's not a gallery—

Walker It was an Italian restaurant then—for some reason they're still—I got coffee there, the gallery serves—

Nan It's still some kind of restaurant; they've just added art.

Walker I can't tell what it is. They gave me a cigar! The building's the same, though—Ned and Lina must have eaten there, don't you think? With the red-checkered breadsticks and melting Chianti bot—oh! And the two stores next to it were one building and maybe empty—there's all this stuff covering old stuff and old stuff that's been scraped away to reveal older stuff—Look! (*Turning back inside.*)
The drafting table!
This must have been Ned's and Theo's studio, too. They must have designed the house here, don't you think? This must have been the hovel they were living in when they laid the plans for that paradise—

Nan Walker, we shouldn't be here—

Walker It's *ours*!
Nan, it was the weirdest feeling, walking in the first time.

14

The place is so nothing. I couldn't imagine why he'd kept it. I paced the floor for two days, screaming at the walls: "Speak! Speak!" It was infuriating.

Nan We should go somewhere—you need to eat—

Walker This place made as little sense as anything else. Finally, last night, I couldn't sleep, I felt something against my back, under the mattress, no, it *was* "The Princess and the Pea," I rolled off the bed, reached under and found *this:* (*He extracts a notebook.*)
It's a kind of diary, a journal. The inevitable journal! I think that's why he kept this place, it's The House of the Journal. I've been poring over it, my brain's all ragged, I can't make head or tale of it, but it seems to cover *everything:* when they built the house, everybody getting married, births, institutionalizations, etcetera—it *seems* to—it's practically written in cipher. And there are whole bunches of years covered by a single sentence. Still. (*Nan is staring at the journal.*) I know. It gives off an infernal *glow,* doesn't it?

Nan Put it away.

Walker You're cracked.

Nan Put it away now.

Walker We have to read this together, Nan; it insists.

Nan Walker—

Walker (*Firm.*) We *are* reading this today.
I've been away but now I'm back.
We're going to read this and then we're going to the lawyer's and receive what's been left us.
What we should have had a year ago, but for me.
This is the day, Nan.
We're finally going to find out what belongs to us.
(*Lights.*)

Nan (*Solo.*) Plans for the building that would come to be known as Janeway House were completed sometime in the fall of 1960. Ground was broken in early spring of the following year, and my grandparents moved into their new home that winter.

The house was begun modestly, but became instantly famous when it was chosen for the cover of one of the tonier architectural quarterlies of the day—

Walker It became famous when the picture was published in *LIFE*—

Nan It was published first in—

Walker But it only became *famous* when it was published in *LIFE*—

Nan Either way.

I never learned, quite, the technical reasons that the house is great—my brother is better on those, Walker has actually studied that stuff—

Walker I'm not going to go into it—

Nan —but it has something to do with fenestration—

Walker Not really—

Nan —and the solids and the, the alternation of solids and—

Walker (*Overlapping.*)—*voids*—the solids and the voids—

Nan And there's a kind of miracle about the light—

Walker All the glass, the house is a prism, but you don't broil in it in the summer—

Nan —and there's a different kind of light in every room, and at every hour—and the rooms themselves have something liquid about them, something that changes. A great writer—I don't remember his name—

Walker (*To assure us.*) But he was German—

Nan —defined architecture as "frozen music."

Walker This is the quality the plans don't capture—

Nan According to the monograph writers, when you look at them, they're very fine, but they somehow don't imply the house itself. Apparently, that's how it is sometimes with great buildings—

Walker There's an intuition held in reserve, a secret the architect keeps until the building is built. It may only be that the plans actually work.

Nan It's also said that of the great houses of the last forty years, this is the best one for living in. . . .

My parents married because it was 1960 and one had to and they were there. And I don't think that's a contemptible thing—for people who have reached a certain age and never found anything better.

I mean, forget about what happened later, think of the *moment.* My mother was lovely, but not as young as she should have been, my father was virtually silent, and they *found* each other and I don't think that's so cynical. He was presentable and serious and he must have seemed calming to her, and solid, and easy to ignore, but not in a bad way. And he was from New England and later New York, so he probably thought she wasn't crazy, just Southern. And if it was calculating, it was a calculation against loneliness, against . . . the possibility of no life at all.

On May 12th, 1972, at around eight P.M., I was in the kitchen of our eleven-room apartment on the Upper East Side, finishing up the dishes and humming. We were living then in a terrible skyscraper my father had designed, his first skyscraper—

Walker —his first building after Theo died—

Nan My brother, who was eight, was in his pajamas, on the living room floor, erecting cities out of this super-sophisticated Tinker Toy kind of thing my father had made for us. My father sat in a large, uncomfortable Modern chair, flipping silently through an art book—

Walker We had dined *à trois* that night because at around seven, my mother had stationed herself in the middle of the long foyer, and for the hour since had been rocking on her haunches, muttering in a private language of her own invention.

Nan I had done with the dishes and was moving onto the water glasses when something happened. The first indication I had was the sound of my brother laughing. He later told me he hadn't reacted to anything new, he'd just looked up and in an instant really seen what was happening—

Walker And I lost it. I mean, it was uncontrollable. Anyway, this triggered something in my mother so she just dashed out of there. She flew out the apartment and down the thousands of flights of stairs all the way to the lobby.

Nan My brother pursued her but couldn't catch her—

Walker There was, I'm sure, an amphetamine involved—

Nan He did arrive in time however to see her body pierce the glass facade of the building—

Walker It was incredible! Straight through. There was this moment, before the blood started, when she looked like something crystal. Then *bam!*—colorized—this sudden redness—everywhere—

Nan My brother was eight years old.
    Meanwhile, upstairs, my father, acting on a hunch, instructed me to telephone for an ambulance while he joined in the chase. I called the ambulance, dried the glasses from

dinner, and sat on the long, steep, uncomfortable couch. Waiting. I was ten.

Sometimes, I ask people, "So how did all of this happen?" and they say, "Oh well, your poor mother, you know, and then, it *was* the sixties."

At any rate.

My mother was taken to the hospital where they did very good work. My brother ran away, but only as far as the laundry room of our building, where he hid in a closet for ten hours until someone thought to check there. My brother returned, my mother returned. Nobody said anything. And it was over.

(*Lights.*)

Walker (*Reading from journal.*) "May 12, 1972: A terrible night."

Nan Walker, stop.

Walker No—I am *not* making this up:
"May 12, 1972: A terrible night."
That evening—

Nan Yes—

Walker This is the only sentence he devotes to it. In my delirium, I thought maybe a page was missing, but no, the subsequent entry is right in place: "May 13, 1972: Food at New York Hospital surprisingly edible."

Nan Please—

Walker I mean, it really is the most extraordinary document. The first thing you notice when you start reading is the style: It doesn't have one. And it manages to sustain that for hundreds of pages—you flip through—narratives of the most wrenching events, and the affect is entirely flat—wait—listen to this—winter of 1966—you know, when Theo is going under?

Listen to our father's rendering:

"January 3rd—Theo is dying."

"January 5th—Theo is dying."

"January 18th"—(I'll skip a little)—"Theo dead."

I mean! His partner. Best and oldest friend: "Theo dying, Theo dying, Theo dead." You could sing it to the tune of "Ob-La-Di."

And it's all like that. Every entry. Years and years of—wait—this is the best of all—the first note—the kickoff, you'll—listen:

"1960, April 3rd to April 5th—Three days of rain." (*Beat.*) Okay. Look. Let's—

Reconstruct along with me a moment. You are this young man. Ambitious, of course—what architect isn't ambitious? And it's that moment when you're so bursting with feeling that people aren't enough, your art isn't enough, you need something else, some other way to let out everything that's in you. You buy this notebook, this volume into which you can pour your most secret, your deepest and illicit passions. You bring it home, commence—the first sacred jottings—the feelings you couldn't contain:

"April 3rd to April 5th: Three days of rain." A weather report. *A fucking weather report!* (*Beat. He quiets down.*)

You know, the thing is with people who never talk, the thing is you always suppose they're harboring some enormous secret. But, just possibly, the secret is, they have *absolutely nothing to say.* (*Beat.*)

Anyway, I want you to give me the house.

Nan What?

Walker I want the house. I want to buy your share in—

Nan You hated him. Why do you want his house?

Walker Because I don't live anywhere.

Oh, look, look, I can't be sure of this but I think when I got lost this last time, when I disappeared, it was so that you would find me.

I know that makes me an impossible person, I *am* an impossible person, it's fact, but, anyway, when all those months passed and no one showed up, I started to believe you had forgotten me. I don't mean as in "ceased to care," I mean as in, "couldn't place the name." That's absurd, but I was living in a country where I didn't speak the language and it started to seem truly possible. Crazy—but that's not exactly foreign terrain for us, is it? I really started to believe I was going—crazy, I—

Nan (*Softly.*) Sweetie—

Walker The reason I don't like being around people who are like me only old is that they always seem to be ending so badly.
I don't want to end badly.
And I don't want to be this burden on people I love so much.
And the house is very beautiful. I think it could only have been designed by someone who was happy. And I'd like to believe that was part of it, too.
The city—it's dangerous to me. It's let me . . . become nothing.
I want to be sane. I want a place that belongs to me.
Let me have the house. Please. (*Beat.*)

Nan Put away the book.

Walker . . . But—

Nan Put away the book and never take it out again. The house for the book. That's my offer. (*A hesitation. Walker replaces the journal beneath the mattress.*) And that's the end of it.

Walker Yes. Thank you.

Nan Now let's go or we really will be late.

Walker Yes, yes . . . let me get my coat.

Nan I'll wait outside. (*She goes out. Walker puts on his coat, retrieves the book, buries it in a pocket, joins her outside.*) You're ready?

Walker Absolutely.

Nan. You'll come all the time, won't you? It'll be everyone . . .

Nan Of course. Let's go. We don't want to leave Pip alone
with the lawyer.

Walker God, no—he might try to work out a side deal! (*They
leave. Lights.*)

(*The sound of car brakes squealing. Pip rushes on, as
though late, slams door behind him, catches his breath,
smiles at audience.*)

Pip (*Solo.*) Hi. Hello. Okay: now me.

My name is Phillip O'Malley Wexler—well, Pip to those
who've known me a little too long. My father, the architect
Theodore Wexler, died of lung cancer at the age of thirty-
eight, even though he was the only one of his generation who
never smoked. I was three when it happened, so, of course, I
forgot him instantly. My mother tried to make up for this by
obsessively telling me stories about him, this kind of rolling
epic that trailed me through life, but they, or *it*, ended up
being mostly about her. Which was probably for the best.

Anyway, it went like this:

My mother, Maureen O'Malley back then, came to New
York in the spring of '59. She was twenty, her parents staked
her to a year, and she arrived with a carefully-thought-out
plan to be amazing at something. Well, the year went by
without much happening and she was miserable because she
was afraid she was going to have to leave New York and
return, in disgrace, to Brooklyn.

Early one morning, after a night when she couldn't sleep at
all, she started wandering around the city. It was raining, she
had her umbrella, she sat in the rain under her umbrella on a
bench in Washington Square Park, and felt sorry for herself.
Then she saw my father for the first time.

"There he was," she told me, "this devastatingly handsome man"—that was an exaggeration, he looked like me—and he was obviously, miraculously, even *more* unhappy than she was. He was just thrashing through the rain, pacing and thrashing, until, all at once, he stopped and sank onto the bench beside her. But not because of her. He didn't realize she was there. He didn't have an umbrella so my mother shifted hers over to him.

"Despair," my mother told me, "can be attractive in a young person. Despair in a young person can be seductive."

Well, eventually she got tired of him not noticing the wonderful thing she was doing for him so she said, a little too loudly:

"Can I help you? May I be of help to you?"

Because he'd been crying.

And he jumped! Man, he *shrieked*!

But he stayed anyway, and they talked, and I was born, the end.

Okay. So, my mother had been telling me that story for about ten years before it occurred to me to ask: "Why was he crying? What was my father so upset about the first time he met you?" "I never knew," she said. He just told her he was fine, she took him to breakfast, they talked about nothing, and I guess she kind of gawked at him. And the more she gawked, I guess the happier he felt, because by the end of breakfast it was as if nothing had happened and they were laughing and my mother was in love and the worst day of her life had become the best day of her life.

When she first came to New York, my mother would stay up till dawn debating Abstract Expressionism and *Krapp's Last Tape,* and then she'd sneak out to a matinee of one of those plays you could never remember the plot of where the girl got caught in the rain and had to put on the man's bathrobe and they sort of did a little dance around each other and fell in love. And there wasn't even a single good joke, but my mother would walk out after and the city seemed dizzy with this absolutely random happiness, and that's how she met my father.

She's hardly ever home anymore. She travels from city to city.

I think she's looking for another park bench, and another wet guy. That's okay. I hope she finds him. (*Lights. Walker sits outside the apartment building. Nan and Pip are inside. Nan is seated in the window, quite still. Pip paces.*)

Nan I know, Pip.

Pip I mean, it's incredible, I mean, I can't believe it!

Nan I know that, yes—

Pip It's the same thing all over again—it's the same thing, Nan—

Nan I know—

Pip I mean, when Walker was gone, all I could remember was all the great things about him. Which when you think about it is a pretty meager amount of material to spread out over a year—

Nan I—yes—

Pip Well, I mean, no, not really, but this stuff, this stuff! I mean, you'd think returning from the dead would be character-improving, but I mean: Look at him. He *chooses* to *sit* there in the pretty cold *evening*, and, somehow, *I* feel guilty about it! As if I were the weather! Or something. I mean—

Nan Yes—

Pip What he said to me, Jesus, at the *lawyer's*! He's *my* lawyer, too, you know. Can you imagine how *chagrined* I'll be next time I have to—okay, not that I ever really need to use him, so it's not that bad, I guess—but still to be the victim of

this—Shakespearean tirade—or at least Maxwell Anderson--
as if I'd *done* something—which I haven't—but still I feel
guilty about it because he's in *so much pain.* You know?

Nan Yes, I—

Pip And I'm really hungry—I haven't eaten anything but star
fruit all day—but we have to wait while he *sits*—in the cold
for which I am responsible—for him to gather his wits and tell
us it's all right to eat. And I feel *bad* because he's in *so much
pain*—

Nan Yes—

Pip I mean, it was a terrible thing—I guess—what happened
there—

Nan It was—

Pip It was a brutal thing—in a way—and I feel awful about
it—but it's something that a dead man—may he rest in peace,
God rest his soul—did—and I'm sorry to refer to your father
that way but—

Nan "Dead man" is all right—

Pip —but I didn't do it. And Walker is great, I mean, don't
get me wrong, Walker is great. He's great. Sometimes I
question Walker's greatness, but he's great . . . and he's in *so
much pain*—but to *call me* things like that in front of all the
wood and the leather and the lawyer—it's really inexcusable,
it's incorrigible. And you can't say anything to him. You can't
scream at him, you can't disapprove of him, you can't even,
you know, mildly *remonstrate* with him because he's in *so
much pain.*

Nan Yes.

Pip I mean, has there ever been a time when he wasn't in *so
much pain*?

Nan No.

Pip No, I mean, I remember when we were *ten,* not doing things because he was in *so much pain.* I connected everything to it: "I better not eat that baloney sandwich, Walker is in *so much pain.*" I mean, a ten-year-old boy shouldn't be so emotionally, whatever, *fastidious* about another ten-year-old boy's feelings, but, with *him.* . .

Nan I know.

Pip There comes a time, Nan, there just comes a point when you have to say: Enough, I don't care that you're in so much pain, you cannot behave like this any longer. (*Beat.*) But you can't because he's in *so much pain.*

Nan I know.

Pip I didn't do anything like what he accused me of, Nan, I didn't manipulate anything; you believe that, don't you?

Nan Can we talk about something else?

Pip Shit.

Nan How are you, or something? We haven't had a chance to—

Pip Nan.

Nan Oh look, we're *stuck* here, you know, we're—and I haven't spoken to you in too long and I've *missed you,* so can't we just . . . how *are* you? (*Beat.*) Please. (*Beat. Pip takes a breath, relaxes, smiles.*)

Pip Well . . . you know . . . I'm great, mostly. Mostly I'm great.

Nan I'm glad. . . . And Maureen?

Pip Mom's doing good, thank you. She sends a big hello from Prague, by the way. And your mother? (*Nan raises an eye-*

brow.) Sorry. (*Nan looks at him, starts to smile*.) What . . . what?

Nan I watch you on that show.

Pip That's mortifying.

Nan When I don't have anything in the afternoon. There you are . . . shirtlessly . . . doing things.

Pip Are you ashamed of me?

Nan Ashamed?

Pip When you watch, does it make you—

Nan It makes me smile, to see you.

Pip That's what I'll think of tomorrow, when I'm taping.

Nan You enjoy it, don't you?

Pip I do, I really do. I mean, I really do. People recognize me. Well, "Butte," anyway. And they treat me well, they *give* me things—because of this ridiculous part, it's wild!

Nan I can't imagine it's much of a *chal*lenge though.

Pip Well, you know, I think for a really *great* actor it wouldn't be? But for me it sort of is?

Nan You're a very good actor.

Pip No, I'm not.

Nan You *are*—that thing you did we saw that time, that was very—

Pip No, no it's okay. I don't need to be some great actor. That just makes it even more magical somehow, you know that I'm doing so well when I'm really so *eh*. I don't need bucking up. I see these other people on the show in their dressing rooms with their little Signet editions of *Pericles, Prince of Tyre*, or whatever, *studying*. And it's so pathetic.

27

These people shouldn't be studying, they should be *investing*. But you can't say anything to them because they're Persons of the Theatre, they go to *class*. I'm so lucky! I can't believe it! I get to go to great restaurants, I pick up the check, pretty girls will date me, I eat chocolate and never gain weight, life is *good* . . .

Nan Good.

Pip And you? I mean, other than the obvious?

Nan . . . Yes, fine. No, lovely, truly.

Pip Milly must, be, like, four-and-a-half now?

Nan Yes. Exactly.

Pip And Nick, I know, last-week-I-sent-the-toy, he's just three.

Nan Yes. They're fantastic.

Pip That's great. And Harry?

Nan He's—

Pip He's the best person.

Nan Well, he's—

Pip I'm sorry, unless you can't stand him anymore or something, in which case: *feh*.

Nan No. He *is* the best person.

Pip I always thought that. Does he still have his hair?

Nan . . . Yes.

Pip That, too!

Nan Uh-huh. He's quite amazing.
    He always says the right thing.

Pip . . . Okay.

Nan No, I don't mean it like that, I don't mean the socially *grace*ful thing—sometimes he will say the very opposite of the—that can be *har*rowing when that happens but . . . he's just so *kind,* do you know?

So unbelievably . . . (*She looks at Pip.*)

He's what *you* would be if—

Pip If I had substance?

Nan If I hadn't met you till I was twenty-five.

Pip Then when you think of me, it's not with unbridled scorn?

Nan Not unbridled.

Pip Mingled with affection?

Nan *You,* Phillip, are my role model.

Pip (*Smiles, a bit shy.*) Thank you.

Listen, I'm just going, I'm starving, I'm gonna get something at that new cigar bar across the street—I think I read they serve food; so what if I have to walk past him? Can I get you something? Or will you come or—

Nan I'll wait.

Pip I'll be back in a— (*Heading out, Pip bumps into Walker, who's heading in.*) Oh. Hey.

Walker Hello. (*Silence. They all arrange themselves in the room.*)

Pip I was just—do you want to go get food?

Walker I'm not actually hungry. If you are, you can—

Pip No, that's fine, I'm fine. (*Beat. Silence. Walker looks to Nan.*)

Walker I'm very sorry, Pip. What I said to you at the lawyers was really, really awful.

Pip Wow.

Walker It's just, you see, when the thing happened . . . it was unbearable.

Pip Oh sure, I mean, yeah.

Walker (*Overlapping.*) It was really excruciating and—

Pip Well, it must have been—

Walker And I, typically made it into this vast, sort of Oedipal saga, totally over the top—

Pip (*Overlapping from "over the top."*) Which is a story that doesn't even make sense when you think about it, but no, Walker, this is really terrific—

Walker (*Overlapping.*) and I realize that I was wrong—what?

Pip What?

Walker *What* doesn't make sense?

Pip What? Oh, nothing.

Walker You said something doesn't—

Pip No, I, no. I just want to thank you for apologizing. I know that's not easy for you and—

Nan "Oedipus" doesn't make sense?

Walker That *is* what he said. In what way doesn't "Oedipus" make sense?

Pip Oh, no, I, that was, I don't want to get into it. (*But they're staring at him.*) No, I mean, just from a practical point of view, not in any deep-structural way or . . . anything. (*Beat.*) No, I mean, it's just, like . . . if some oracle told you you were going to kill your father and marry your mother, wouldn't you just never kill anybody and stay single? . . . And then, if you *did* inadvertently kill somebody, in the heat of the moment or something, and later started dating? Wouldn't you be smart enough to, like, *avoid older women*? I mean, to me the moral of that story is not your destiny awaits you. To me it's . . . you know . . . Do the Fucking Math. (*Beat.*)

Walker You must publish.

Pip Walker.

Walker It would be a crime if these insights were limited to this room.

Pip Okay, Walker, I wasn't pretending—

Walker No: Really, we must notify the university presses at once to—

Nan All right Walker.

Walker Yes, I meant not to do that.

Pip I walked right into—

Walker You did.

Nan You always do.

Pip I do. I always do. Walker, let me just say it—

Nan Can we go somewhere, can we eat something?

Pip What happened at the lawyer's, doesn't mean your father hated you.

Walker Uumm . . . was that proposed?

Pip I don't know why I got the house.

Walker I don't think I ever said—God! "Hate"—I mean—!

Pip I know that's what has to be going through your head.

Walker Well now it is.

Pip But I'm sure it wasn't that—it wasn't even necessarily insensitive, you know.

Nan (*Involuntary.*) It was wicked. (*A hesitation.*) I said nothing.

Pip You know, it's not as if he disinherited you. You got a fortune, literally a fortune.

Walker That's beside the point.

Pip No, wait, no, that can't be, I mean, there is no point so *huge* that that much money can be *beside* it.

Walker I would have traded it for the house.

Pip That would have been *dumb*.

Walker Oh, Christ.

Pip Look I'm just caught up in this, I'm not the mastermind behind it, I don't even know how it's possible, really, I mean, why didn't it revert to your mom?

Nan He got it in the divorce.

Pip In the divorce?

Nan Yes.

Pip They were divorced?

Nan Oh God.

Pip How did I miss that?

Walker You have your ways.

Nan We were in college. They'd been separated so long by then, it was practically just paperwork. Anyway, it didn't change anything.

Pip I can't believe I—

Nan It doesn't matter.

Pip Anyway, the point is, Walker, you were wrong.

Walker I've already apologized.

Pip Not just wrong to say it: incorrect. Your dad and I—it was not some sort of quasi-paternal "substitution" or "alienation of affection" or whatever you called it. You know what your dad was to me: this nice kind of uncle, I wasn't *working on* him or—

Walker I realize that.

Pip I'd just drop by occasionally, in the afternoons, if I had an audition in the neighborhood or something. It wasn't any big deal.

Walker Yes, I know.

Pip I was just somebody he found it easy to talk to. (*Sudden frigid silence.*)

Walker Ah.

Pip He was a pretty lonely man in the last few years. I don't think he was doing that much work on his own, all the partners were always buzzing around, he'd be twiddling his thumbs. I'd just pop in. I thought it was my responsibility. You were in Boston. *You* were always flittering off to Peru or Weehawken or wherever. We'd sit and gab.

Walker And what would you "gab" about?

Pip We'd—whatever was going on—sports!

Walker ... Sports?

Pip Or anything. Don't ask me for details, it wasn't recorded for posterity, it was just chat—easy, you know?

Walker ... I see.

Pip And I never made a single overture about the house. I, the ironic part is, I can't even use the house, really; frankly, I don't even like it much.

Walker You don't *like* it much?

Pip No.

Walker That's not acceptable.

Pip It's just my opinion.

Walker You don't get to have an opinion.

Pip I got the *house*. I think I should be allowed to express a point of view—

Walker That doesn't follow.

Pip Look, it's not that I think it's *bad* work, I just find it a little stark.

Walker Stark.

Pip Yes.

Walker Stark!

Pip Yes!

Walker Well, what do you know? Before you favored us with your views on Greek Tragedy, and now we get to hear you hold forth on Architecture as well. I never before realized you were a cultural critic of such extreme *scope*—

Pip Don't start.

Walker No, no, I want *more*, I want to hear you on, you know, Hegel and Umberto Eco—Boolean Algebra—

Pip Walker, stop.

Walker No, it's such a privilege to learn what a TV actor who plays a character named after a geological formation has to *say* about the really important events in world culture—

Nan All right Walker—

Walker I'm especially interested in your visual aesthetic—

Nan Please be quiet.

Walker Because I think the real innovations are going to come from people who buy antiqued Italianate chiffarobes from catalogues.

Pip You're not exactly one to comment on anyone's environment, Walker.

Walker Oh, really?

Pip After where you were living, that apartment.

Walker That—?

Pip I mean, really: interior decoration by Jeffrey Dahmer.

Walker You saw where I was—

Pip I was your "in case of emergency" contact. So don't get hoity-toity about it. I swear, it was horrible, it was crazy, I thought it was your mom all over again.

Walker We would love you to be silent, now.

Pip I mean, why do you get to be the one who judges things when you're having the stupidest life of anybody? I'm sick of it, Walker. *You're* the one who's done the bad thing here, you're the one who ran off like a maniac and left us to go bonkers worrying about you. I've been good, Nan's been good, you've been bad. Okay, that's the morality of the situation. So you don't get to make the laws; that's the upshot.

Walker I wish—

Pip No, *I'm* talking now, and it's a very weird sensation. Look, Walker, look—it's just you can't be the only personality in the room anymore. You cannot just change the temperature of every circumstance by this kind of tyrannical psychosocial, you know, *fiat—oh, look,* I know you think I'm an idiot—

Walker I never said you were an idiot.

Pip Yes, you did, you said it all the time, you just pretended sometimes not to mean it; but I know you meant it.

Walker I didn't.

Pip Even though *I* was the one who was off the charts in any standardized exam we ever took, while you were always getting *lost* on the way to the *test*ing center. But that doesn't matter, I know—with your exquisite perversity that just *proves* it, but look, the fact is, it isn't true—being in a good mood is not the same thing as being a moron. It just isn't. And, you know, for years I wondered. I strove to sustain some level of unhappiness because I felt so left out but I couldn't manage it—

Walker I never intended you to—

Pip I don't know—I feel bad—I go to the gym—I feel better. Maybe that means I lack *gravitas* or something, but the hell with it, I'm having a good time.

Walker I'm glad for—

Pip Except I am no longer willing to bear the brunt of your *mean*ness.

Walker I'm sorry, I—

Pip You know, it's not as if I don't know where it's coming from, it's not as if I don't know you've always been basically in love with me—that's been so obvious for so many years that—

Walker Oh Jesus—Jesus—

Pip I don't know what—but why does it have to be such a problem? Why couldn't we have just worked it through when we were eighteen? It would have been so easy. I would have been sensitive, you would have suffered for a while, it would have been over, and we could have spent the next fifteen years going to the movies or something like *people*. Instead of it fucking up everything.

Walker This is a little too—

Pip Because it's just fucked up everything for such a long time—everything we had to keep from you—

Nan Pip.

Pip ... the stupid, gothic secrets—the tiptoeing around—

Nan Pip.

Pip I mean, like all that time when Nan and I were sleeping together and in love and everything and we couldn't tell you because we were so afraid of how jealous you'd be, and we couldn't tell each other why we couldn't tell you because nobody was acknowledging any aspect of the situation—it was crazy, that felt awful—I hated lying to you. Like it or not, you're my oldest friend. I love you, you know, and what was the point? Everything is tolerable if you just *talk* about it, you know? (*Beat. Silence between Walker and Nan.*) You know? (*Beat.*) Was that *all* new information?

Walker I'm going to get something to eat at the place. Don't come there, okay? (*He exits.*)

Pip Oh. Oh damn. I had no idea. That was such a long time ago, I assumed—do things really stay secret that long? (*Beat.*) Nan?

Nan Well, it's a stupid thing. It's just a stupid thing.

Pip It's nothing at this point, isn't it? We were, like, eighteen years old, even *his* statute of limitations must have run out by now. This won't be a big deal.

Nan It will go on forever. (*Beat. Looks at her watch.*) I'm not going to make it home to put my kids to bed.

Pip If you catch the next shuttle—

Nan I won't catch the next shuttle. (*Pause.*) What was hard when he finally called, what was hard was to realize he was still alive. For the first . . . nine months, I think, every day I woke up in a panic—if I'd slept—with these unbearably vivid pictures of what had befallen him. And I'd go through most of the day mourning. Then it would occur to me that what I was so certain had happened to him almost certainly had not happened to him—the mere fact of my inventing it had made it unlikely— and there would be a momentary, I don't know, *rest,* I suppose. And I'd go on to imagine some other horrible thing.

Then . . . it stopped.

I don't know how. I realized it afterward—some *weeks* afterward—I was on to other things. I was back . . . with my children. I was back in the day. At home. In Boston. And it was sad, but better. It was much better.

What I mean is, when I heard his voice again the main feeling was not relief. (*Pause.*)

Today, when he asked for the house, I thought, oh God, yes, take the house, let him have it, the house will take care of him. And I'll be free. (*Beat.*) Do you want to get something to eat? I've got a lot of time to kill.

Pip I'll give him the house.

Nan You can't do that.

Pip Why not? It's mine, I can do whatever I want with it.

Nan You can't do that for him.

Pip Well, in the first place I'm doing it for you—

Nan God, that's—

Pip . . . and, second, I don't even really want it and he needs it, and I, well, really can't stand to think of you un—you know—happy, and I've got the solution so—hey: Christmas!

Nan You cannot *give* it away. Do you have any idea how much that house is worth?

Pip Okay, then I'll sell it to him; that's even better.

Nan But—

Pip He can afford it after all the money he got—you, too! Good God, am I the only one who realizes this was a *good day*?

Nan Do you *mean* this?

Pip Yes!

Nan Can I go tell him now?

Pip Yes. And then I'll take you to the airport.

Nan I—what?

Pip If we leave in ten minutes, you can make the plane.

Nan . . . Pip.

Pip That's my stipulation.

Nan I—

Pip Or the deal is off.

Nan But—

Pip I will sell him the house, but you have to go home.

Nan You are . . . (*She can't find the word for his wonderfulness.*)

Pip (*Accepting the compliment.*) Yes, I am. Go! (*Nan heads out. Pip stays behind a moment. Looks at the room. He touches the surface of the drafting table. Something like a shudder goes through him. Nan reenters.*)

Nan He's gone.

Pip . . . Are you—? Did you look every—?

Nan It's a tiny place—he's gone off.

Pip We can get a cab at the corner.

Nan I can't leave without even—he's God-knows-where—

Pip It doesn't make a difference.

Nan Pip—

Pip You can pretend he's dead. (*Beat.*) He's dead, Nan. (*Long pause.*)

Nan Let me have a minute.

Pip I'll get the cab. (*Pip heads outside. She looks around, indecisive. She lifts up the mattress. There's nothing underneath it.*)

Nan God*damn* him! (*Blackout.*)

> (*Late that night. The apartment is dark. Walker enters. Nan is in darkness, curled up on the mattress.*)

Nan Hello. . .

Walker Oh, Jesus! (*He flips on the lights.*) You're still here.

Nan I fell asleep.

Walker I figured you'd gone.

Nan Oh. I almost did. I *should* have. I didn't.

Walker I'm glad.

Nan I turned around at the last minute. I almost made it to the bridge.

Walker Pip—?

Nan . . . went home.

Walker Ah. (*Beat.*)

Nan Where did you go?

Walker I was—every corner of this city—it was—I . . . couldn't stop moving. I tried to calm myself. I . . . got coffee at a couple of—that was a bad idea—I ended up counting the Wexler Janeway buildings I passed; that was no help at all. I stopped at fourteen.

Nan Fourteen! You must have been to Brooklyn.

Walker I was to—Staten Island!

Nan Jesus.

Walker Not very young, not very merry, but I rode back and forth for hours on the—

Nan What time is it, anyway?

Walker I have no idea; did you ever eat?

Nan No.

Walker (*Burrowing in his rucksack, pulling out a paper bag.*) I've got—I picked up this stuff from a deli tray. It's probably still all right. (*Opens the bag.*)

Nan What is it?

Walker I think either tiramisu . . . or squid.

Nan I pass. (*Beat.*)

Walker Thank you for staying. (*She nods.*) So . . . we don't have to talk about it.

Nan Thank *you*.

Walker . . . So how long did it go on?

Nan Walker—

Walker Was it *fun*, was he *good*, what—

Nan I don't want to discuss it.

Walker Okay.

Nan I'm sorry that I kept it from you all this time.

Walker No, that's all right. Actually, it feels quite invigorating to be apologized *to* for a change, that doesn't happen very oft—*tell me,* at least, did it make you happy?

Nan It was a long time ago.

Walker Uh-huh. . .

Nan It was just . . . so easy.

Walker (*Wistfully.*) Oh.

Nan Pip is . . . well-adjusted to the world.

Walker Oh God, well-adjusted? He's precision-manufactured; it's—

Nan *Were* you in love with him?

Walker Oh, who knows? You know, he's such a dunce, I envied him.

Nan Yes. (*Smiles.*) Yes.

Walker Nan, I took the book.

Nan I know that.

Walker I'm a completely untrustworthy person.

Nan Yes.

Walker So I was—anyway—I was reading in it?

Nan Don't tell me—

Walker It was incredible!

Nan It's always incredible—

Walker When Pip, when he said our father hated us—

Nan He said the opposite—

Walker —I couldn't get it out of my head—

Nan —besides he was talking about you, not us—

Walker I thought: Penetrating Simplicity strikes again! Then I saw this bit I hadn't seen before—

Nan Don't read it to me—

Walker I was at this wine and cheese bar—do you believe it? I found the last extant wine and—unless, it's the first *retro* wine and—anyway, they had candlelight, and this one section that I had thought was just a stain suddenly turned out to be *words*— Complete serendipity! Something about the angle of the page and the flame—like a palimpsest or pentimento or whatever you call—I had the most astonishing epiphany.

Nan Your epiphanies never mean anything—

Walker This is important—please!

Nan (*Quietly.*) . . . All right.

Walker It comes after "Theo dead." You know the punch-line of the "Theo dying" series? You have to sort of tilt the page—well, you still can't really—that's all right, I've memorized it—it says: "Theo dead. Everything I've taken from him . . ."
Isn't that extraordinary?

Nan Huh.

Walker It's about the house, you know?

Nan I don't—

Walker No! Listen! Think about it!
Two people work together and in the end, there's no way of telling who's responsible for what. But after Theo died,

nothing Ned did was any good, you see? He just coasted for thirty years. But the early stuff . . . the house . . . do you see? He didn't—you see, this is, this is *it*—he couldn't give it to us because it was never really *his*. It was all Theo's—so he left it to Pip—it's his confession, do you—"Theo dead. Everything I've taken from him." I mean it's so *so* obvious, now. That we never figured this out before!

I like to think that was kind of us.

When I realized, Nan, I started to see everything backwards through it, everything changed. It began to seem almost as if he weren't even really silent, just talking in that language I think they must use in hell, with everybody signaling wildly all the time, and no one ever picking up on any of it—do you—

Nan It's not necessarily conclusive, you know.

Walker I think it is.

Nan But it's—

Walker I *want* it to be. (*Beat.*)

Nan All right. Then it can be.

Walker Thank you. (*Beat.*)

Nan Pip wants to give you the house.

Walker He wants to—?

Nan *Sell* you, rather; he wants to sell you the house.

Walker Why?

Nan He thinks it would be good for you to have it. He *wanted* to give it to you, but I—

Walker Christ, he's unreal!

Nan I know—anyway I persuaded him to—

Walker It's like he comes from this weird other *nice* species or—

Nan I persuaded him to take money—

Walker Thank God.

Nan So. You will call him tomorrow—no: I will call him for you, and I will call Mr. Fisher, and we will set up a meeting to which you will show up promptly, and wearing a nice suit, and you will . . . have the house.

Walker I don't want it anymore.

Nan I wish I were *dead*.

Walker No.

Nan I wish I were dead—

Walker You don't—

Nan I wish . . . *you* were.

Walker That makes sense. . . . It's not the same house anymore, do you know?

Nan . . . Where will you live? Where are you . . . going to go tomorrow morning? Where—

Walker I thought here.

Nan . . . This place?

Walker For a while.

Nan *Look* at this place.

Walker Until I find something out of the city.

Nan It's no place.

Walker It's sort of random; I like that.

Nan (*Looking around.*) Oh God . . .

Walker What?

Nan I'm just trying to picture how you can possibly make this room look any worse.

Walker (*Enthusiastically.*) I *can*.
  Nan, we need to have a service!

Nan What kind of a—

Walker I missed my father's funeral—Jesus! That's shocking! We need to do something.

Nan That's all right.

Walker We *do*—what, though? It's so hard to improvise something ancient and sacred.

Nan It's impossible.

Walker No—yes—we can do it—all we need is a couple of props—

Nan Like what?

Walker Fire.

Nan Oh God, Walker, please don't burn down this building.

Walker I have the cigar! (*He finds matches.*)

Nan Don't light that—I haven't eaten—the smell—

Walker That's okay, if you throw up, it will be ceremonial. (*He goes to light the cigar, interrupts himself.*) Wait—no— first . . . (*He lays the book open on the table.*) Say good-bye . . .

Nan That's . . . corny.

Walker Come on, Nan. Say good-bye to the dead.

Nan (*A moment. Then softly.*) . . . Good-bye.

Walker Good-bye. (*A moment. Walker puts the cigar in his mouth, takes out matches, strikes a match, brings it to the cigar; wavers for a second, then suddenly, sharply, puts the match to the book.*)

Nan Jesus!

Walker Better get some water in case this thing grows—

Nan Jesus, Walker—put that out—before the whole book is gone—

Walker Too late now—

Nan Oh God—this is crazy—

Walker I feel like Hedda Gabler!

Nan Goddamn you, Walker—now we'll never know anything! (*They watch the book burn.*)

Fade out. End Act One.

Act Two

1960

The setting is the same, only enhanced, filled with color now, and the apartment has furniture.

In the apartment: Ned is quietly sketching. When he finishes a sketch, he looks at it, tears it up calmly, and throws it away; then he does it all again.

After a moment, Theo and Lina round the street corner, arguing. They stop outside the building.

Theo Don't, Lina! Do not change the subject. Do not avoid the point like this—

Lina I am avoiding nothing; there is no point, there never is with you, Theo—

Theo What incredibly noisy crap that—

Lina It *is* a choice. Either you consecrate yourself to this *vie de bohème* existence of yours or you—

Theo Jargon! Rhetoric!

Lina —or simply acknowledge that you're a young man on the make as surely as if you were working for the House of Morgan and your *architecture* is just a vehicle for your rise—

Theo (*Overlapping from "vehicle."*) What this has to do with that trashy little display you put on—at the *Plaza* for Christ's—

Lina I couldn't stand her, okay! I couldn't stand that little Farmington witch with her—Peter Pan collars and her—little string of pearls—

Theo Witch? She's a girl reporter! Ten minutes out of Mt. Holyoke or someplace! She was *inter*viewing me. She's just this nice girl—

Lina (*Morally conclusive.*) She was wearing gloves!

Theo (*Stymied a second, then.*) . . . At Condé Nast they make them—

Lina Oh, I *bet* they make them at Condé Nast.

Theo —wear *gloves.*

Lina She was gazing the entire time at your—

Theo Do you have only *one* subject?

Lina CROTCH!

Theo *Oh, Jesus!*

Lina And she hated me. She hated me.

Theo She was kind enough, Lina—generous enough to set up this interview—possibly to *place* us among the really important—

Lina Importantly well-connected—

Theo —young creative forces of our time—

Lina You're talking like the Book-of-the-Month Club, Theo. Some drivel in a magazine will not make you Christopher Wren! (*Ned, who has been listening, very still and attentive, puts his hands to his ears. Then he takes a jazz record out of its rack and puts it on the hi-fi to drown them out.*)

Theo I mean, it was *tea* at a nice hotel—why does that have to be *hard*?

Lina (*Overlapping.*) Oh and wasn't *that* an elevating locale? How interesting to discover that you can get a cup of tea at the Plaza for actually *less* than it costs to send twins through Princeton—

Theo We weren't paying, Lina; and it was going along beautifully until you decided you had to *di*late on the wonders of the oral contraceptive. Until you decided the time was ripe for a little Joycean riff right there in the Palm Court with the *stained glass flowers.* (*Ned turns up the music some more. Theo and Lina hold their own.*)

Lina She had heard it all before, that one.

Theo Oh please—she's from this *family*—she reads expurgated Jane Austen.

Lina You know nothing. (*They're getting louder.*)

Theo God! You have me in this continuous carom between— (*Ned turns music up even more.*)

Lina You know *absolutely nothing*—

Theo ... genital obsession and ethics.

Lina (*Between the eyes.*) You are a naive boy from the suburbs!

Theo I ... (*This stops him. He calls into the apartment.*) Ned! (*Ned pokes his head out the window.*) I mean, would you turn down the music? Jeez, we have *neigh*bors.

Ned ... Sorry. (*He goes back in, turns down music. Theo returns to Lina. Lina looks to him needily. He sighs, turns away a second, then goes back to her, changing the mood, cajoling.*)

Theo Hey ... did you hear this one? (*He sings. Vaguely Lambert, Hendricks and Rossish jazz satire.*)
    Joan of Arc was a woman of convictions
    She never shirked a difficult situation
    She thought she should save France
    So she saved France
    Why can't you be more like that?

(Theo's used the song to move in on her. By the time he's through, he's holding her, kissing her neck. When the song is over, she laughs, reaches to pull his head to hers. They kiss. Ned looks up from drawing, looks out, watches, returns to drawing. When Theo and Lina start bickering again, it's more reined in at first; they're trying to sustain the mood.)

Lina *(Coming out of the kiss.)* Why doesn't anyone know about me?

Theo Oh, *man*! What are you—

Lina Nobody knows about me—

Theo Everyone—

Lina Your parents—why—

Theo Is that what all this has been about?

Lina No! I don't know—I don't—

Theo You know the minute parents come into it, everything changes—

Lina And do we want things to stay like this?

Theo Changes for the worse. Heidegger wrote: "The light of the public always obscures."

Lina Heidegger is a famous Nazi.

Theo In the first place, you don't know. In the second place, you have to separate the work from the—

Lina Oh, what are we *talk*ing about? How wretched you are—using words like Heidegger! Are you ashamed of me?

Theo Christ, can anything happen without me being guilty of it?

Lina No, I didn't . . . you don't . . . let me—

Theo You—

Lina I mean: *Am* I something to be ashamed of?

Theo No—!

Lina No—no—don't be—easy—I *wonder* this . . . I some-times think—

Theo (*Moving in, trying to make it intimate again.*) You think too much—

Lina I would just like something to be—

Theo You think all the time—

Lina I would like something to be . . . authentic, I can never find—

Theo It's such a beautiful night—why can't it just be—

Lina That doesn't matter—

Theo Why can't it just be a beautiful night?

Lina You have to deserve nights like this—

Theo I don't—

Lina I do—

Theo What is this? Racial guilt? The legacy of slaveowners?

Lina What a blithering idiot you are! What a fool, what a dunce! What a nightmare, what a moron! Slaveowners—we—we practically begged table scraps from sharecroppers, we—you—

Theo Lina, please—

Lina What a messed-up, delusional, romantic you are!

Theo I'm . . . I'm going to get a pizza.

Lina Theo? (*He stops.*) I sometimes don't know if I'll get through the night. (*Theo just spreads his arms: "I don't know how to answer that." He starts to walk away.*) Theo? (*He* *pauses.*) Pepperoni. (*He walks off. Lina is left alone. After a moment.*) NED! (*Ned bounds to the window.*)

Ned Y-y-yes?

Lina Are you busy? Are you in the middle of something?

Ned N-n-o.

Lina Do you want to come out and have a cigarette with me?

Ned Y-y-yes.

Lina Come out! . . . Ned?

Ned Y-y-yes?

Lina Bring cigarettes.

Ned Okay. (*He grabs cigarettes, vaults out of the apartment. When they're together.*) H-hi. (*He takes out cigarettes, hands her one.*)

Lina Light, please. (*He lights her cigarette.*) Thank you. (*She smiles. They smoke. Ned is excited to be with her, excruciatingly shy, awkward standing, awkward leaning. She smokes wonderfully.*) You must have heard us—did you hear us caterwauling before?

Ned Ye-ye-ye-no.

Lina The whole neighborhood—what fools we are, what fools. . . . I'm sorry for the disturbance. (*Ned waves it away.*) Also—because of me—it looks as though you're *not* going to be instantly translated to fame and greatness in the pages of a glossy magazine without ever having done anything to deserve it.
   I deeply apologize. (*Ned shrugs.*)
   You don't ever say much, do you?

Ned N-no.

Lina . . . You know, Moses stutter—

Ned M-Moses stuttered, I know.

He had . . . many other fine qualities, though. (*Beat. They smoke. Maybe he should go.*) . . . W-well . . .

Lina No—don't leave me. I don't want to just be standing here alone. Theo's gone to that new Italian dive to get a pizza, just stay a while.

Ned . . . All right. (*They smoke.*)

Lina We're going through a rough patch, you see.

Ned Ev-everybody—

Lina —knows?

Ned —does.

Lina Yes—that too.

It's my fault. I'm a troublemaker.

Ned No—

Lina I am. I . . . wear at him. Too emotional, too—

Ned He . . . doesn't . . . mind, he finds it . . . in-interesting.

Lina . . . Oh . . . (*Quietly.*) It isn't so interesting from inside. . . . Of course, he's no field of flowers, either. He makes as much trouble as I do, he—

Ned He's a . . . h-he's a genius.

Lina Yes . . . Naturally, I know that. I *know* he's a genius. . . . Everybody I've met in this city is a genius. And the ones that aren't are connoisseurs. How do you two manage to get along, anyway?

Ned W-w-w-w-w-w-e-e—

Lina You know, Demosthenes—

Ned Y-y-yes, I know. I know all the great . . . stu-stutterers in hi-history, I have . . . their calendar.

Lina I am sorry.

Ned No.

Lina I'm insupportable.

Ned ... No ...

Lina Is it true you're getting therapy for it? Theo says you're getting therapy for it.

Ned He told you that?

Lina Was he not to? Is it a secret? Are you honing your legend, too, the way Theo does? All charismatic poses and strategic suppressions?

Ned ... I am ... getting therapy.

Lina What does the therapy consist of?

Ned ... Breathing.

Lina Breathing?

Ned She's teaching me to ... b-breathe.

Lina Me, next ...

Ned ... as though it were my ... b-birthright ... she says. *Does* he h-hone his legend?

Lina Doesn't he?

Ned The ... thing about Theo is—

Lina The thing about Theo is he's had a very poor education.

Ned Has, has he?

Lina Yes.

Ned But he's gone to—

Lina Yes, yes, I know the list of schools. It's an embarrass-ing list of schools. But the fact is, he's got *nothing* out of them. He's probably the best-schooled worst-educated young man on the eastern seaboard. So he's making up.

In bed, he *reads*. He reads like a man about to die who believes St. Peter gives a general information pop quiz.

He's very sweet that way, but it bogs you down. Topics get too tender. Everything threatens to reveal the imposture . . .

What did you think the secret about Theo is?

Ned . . . I . . . don't recall . . . (*Pause.*)

Lina But I think without him, I'll die. (*Pause.*)

Ned He-he . . . wants things.

Lina That's true.

Ned I . . . I . . . n-never . . . m-much . . .
Theo *wants*. Wi-without him, I would . . . probably . . .

Lina I know . . .

Ned I n-never . . .
I went to . . . architecture sc-school to . . . kill time.
I . . . liked to draw.
Th-Theo took me up.
Th-this house . . . we would never have—

Lina I know.

Ned He was the b-best thing for me.
It was the b-best thing that hap-happened.

Lina I know.

Ned I . . . would die, too. (*Lina looks at him, kisses him on the cheek, rushes off.*)

Lina Theo! Theo! WHAT'S TAKING SO LONG? (*Lights.*)

(*Evening, a few days later. Ned calmly inspects a series of drawings. Theo hovers.*)

Theo It came to me *whole*. Do you know those moments? No labor, pure vision: Emerson on the I.R.T.

I started sketching right then—that's the wavery lines—anyway, you know how badly I draw, did you ever hear Cole Porter play piano? It's the same thing.

Are you looking, are you thinking, what? Don't talk. *Think*. I'm jabbering, I'll shut up. I tell you, it was such a startling thing when it came to me, I almost resisted it. I'd become comfortable with failing. I know I wasn't failing yet, but I'd started to fear . . . sterility. Delusion. Emptiness.

Don't look at that, that's corrected on the next page, see? Don't look at that, it's poorly drafted, it's a terrible idea, anyway, it stinks, I'm getting rid of it.

Listen, I'll leave you alone, I'll be silent, you'll be silent, we'll both shut up. (*Beat.*)

Why are you so quiet? Do you hate it? Of course, it's incredibly rough and, who knows, it's in progress, it's, we can throw it away. But at least we *have* something to throw away, that's the crucial step, it's when you have something you can reject completely that you know you're almost there. And it's not as if anybody else was coming up with, it's not as if you're—and of course even if it's *genius* it may not be suitable, it may not be suitable to your parents. After all it's your parents' dime we're spending (more or less literally, but) anyway, who knows what their taste is, who knows if they even *have* taste; really, there's no reason to believe they have taste at all . . .

Why are you looking there again? You already looked there. Is something wrong? Look, obviously all the sketches are clumsy, the arithmetic is wrong, the proportions are out of proportion. Can you see the intention though?

Tell me. Tell me the truth. Tell me the absolute truth. Tell me what I want to hear. The absolute truth that I want to hear. Say nothing. *Talk*.

Ned ... It's ...

Theo I know it's rough.

Ned It's ... it's not rough.

Theo But you hate it? It's ugly?

Ned No, it's ... beautiful.

Theo You think that?

Ned I do.

Theo Ned.

Ned I've thought it for y-years.

Theo ... What does that—?
    I don't know what that means.

Ned S-since I first saw it in a magazine.

Theo ... In a ... ?
    Is that *wit*?

Ned Theo, I'm sorry, but it's the Farnsworth House. (*Beat.*)

Theo What are you talking about?

Ned It's the F-Farns—

Theo No, it isn't.
    ... It has elements in *com*mon with the Farnsworth House.

Ned Many el-elements. All of them.

Theo You don't—
    No, you don't underst—

I will grant you—and this was on purpose—that it uses the same vo*cab*ulary—

Ned Theo, if I wrote, "To be or not . . . to be, that is the question," would you tell me it used the same vocabulary as, "To be or not to be, that . . . is the question?"

Theo Look I—
You don't—I—
I would even grant you that it's something of an . . . homage—

Ned Theo, it's not an homage, it's a *copy*. The funny part is, we're . . . all so van-vanguard and when we . . . copy, it's al-always the . . . most obvious p-possible thing. (*Pause.*)

Theo Not "we."

Ned What?

Theo If it's a copy, "we" didn't do it, I did.

Ned . . . Umm . . .
I will t-take responsibility for—

Theo Or take whatever.

Ned What?

Theo No, nothing . . .

Ned Okay.
You . . . don't have an idea, y-yet, that's . . . all right. . . .
My p-parents are p-patient and the m-money's . . . odd jobs.

Theo Mm-hmm. (*Pause. Theo picks up one of his drawings, tears it in two.*)

Ned Well, it's not as if there aren't . . . c-copies in every architecture textbook in the land. (*He picks up pieces.*)
You shouldn't have d-done that, though . . . I'll t-tape it

back together. God, you have a j-juvenile streak a m-mile wide.

Theo Don't bother.

Ned It's not a—

Theo What's the point? I mean, if it's—

Ned It's . . . what you said . . . The . . . thing it will be useful t-to completely . . . discard. That's progress.
It's . . . f-fine to be . . . frustrated . . . but there's t-time.

Theo Not so much time.

Ned Time enough.
D-don't go tearing things up. (*Pause. Theo watches Ned, who doesn't see him.*)

Theo Why do you always do this?

Ned . . . Do . . . *what*?

Theo The thing you always do.

Ned . . . Uumm . . .

Theo What you have done the last, what is it now, seven times I've attempted to—

Ned It's . . . my function.

Theo That's not it.

Ned But it is.
That essay you're . . . forever quoting. Talent is divided into genius and . . . taste. We decided you would be genius and I would be . . . the other. Wh-what we must have been drinking, it's, com-completely embarrassing, but it's how things have worked out.
If they have . . . worked out.

Theo . . . All right.

Ned What?

Theo What?

Ned *What*?
Please don't deliberately n-not . . . say some *one* thing, I—

Theo I'm not.
. . .
It's an incredible evasion, though, isn't it?

Ned What is? How?

Theo Genius and taste—

Ned We were drunk, but it's what—

Theo *When* was this decided?

Ned I don't—it happened.

Theo This . . . division of labor?

Ned Yes.

Theo That I would have ideas and you would destroy them?

Ned That—
Shut up. Just . . . shut up. You're making a f-fool of—

Theo That *is* what happens, though.

Ned . . . If it seems that way, then—

Theo Do you understand how *protected* that is? Do you understand how safe you are?

Ned I—

Theo Is it clear to you—do you recognize that for me everything is at risk and for you nothing?

Ned No.
No, I . . . do not understand that . . .

Listen, it's early enough—don't start.

Maybe this kind of weird, sa-sadistic rite has some kind of ... sexual dividend ... when it's with Lina, but I don't ... like it—

Theo This is another evasion.

Ned If you w-want me to tell you ... bad work is good, I ... I won't do it ... I'd ... rather ... look, why don't you just shut up, now?

Theo I don't want to—

Ned Then ... I'm going to go for a walk.

Theo All you ever do is escape—

Ned ... All right ...

Theo Even the stutter is just another—

Ned (*Overlapping.*) Are you—

Theo —just another form of—

Ned You're out of your mind—

Theo Why am I the one who does the work? Why was this decided?

Ned ... Theo—

Theo Tell me.

Ned You—

Theo Say it.

Ned ...
You have more talent. That's ... a given.
We've known that since ... sc-school. We've known, ev-everybody's known that since ...

Theo And because of that you feel compelled to punish me.

Ned We're . . . p-partners. We're . . . in business toge-to-gether. This house—my p-parents co-commissioned this house—

Theo Also hostile; also a manipulation.

Ned I'm-I'm-I'm-I'm s-sure you . . . could w-walk up and down West End Avenue and a . . . th-thousand psy-psychiatrists would agree with everything you say, but it's g-garbage and I d-don't—

Theo I just want to know why it is I'm the one who has to *pay* in this situation—

Ned Telling s-someone he's . . . more gifted than you . . . costs something—

Theo (*Overlapping.*) *Is* it just envy? And of what? Is it sex? Is it Lina? Is it me?

Ned (*Overlapping.*) I l-left home to get away from people who have no—

Theo (*Overlapping.*) I mean, was the whole point of this some kind of revenge—?

Ned (*Overlapping.*)—p-people who have no g-grace, people who are r-randomly cruel and y-you are—

Theo (*Overlapping.*) I was your friend. I am your friend. You had no other friends, I took you in—

Ned I—

Theo Who else did you have? What else did you have? Where would you be?

Ned I-I—

Theo Tell me—

Ned I-I-I—

Theo *Say* it! Just say it, Ned. *Say it*—

Ned (*He can't get his breath, he can't stop stuttering.*) I-I-I-I-I-I-I . . . (*Theo sees what's happening, is instantly remorseful, sickened.*)

Theo Oh God . . . no, don't . . . no . . . Don't try . . . it's all right . . . I'm sorry . . . I'm . . . (*Theo approaches Ned, not knowing what to do. Theo circles his arms around Ned as if to hold him, but doesn't complete the gesture.*) I'm sorry . . . Forget it . . . Please . . . forget this. . . . Please . . . please . . .

Ned It's . . . all *right!* (*Pause. They move away from each other. Beat.*)

Theo You shouldn't let me do that to you, Ned. You can't let me do that to you.

Ned I'm sorry. (*Pause.*) We d-don't . . . have to k-keep this up.

Theo We do—

Ned N-not if—

Theo What would happen to you?

Ned . . . It's not *Of Mice and Men* . . .

Theo I know that, but . . . you're better off with me.

Ned Yes.
We say that . . . don't we? (*Pause.*)

Theo I'm going to go away for a while. I need to . . .
I'll go to my parents' shack in—

Ned Okay.

Theo Someplace I can work. (*Beat.*) You're right. . . . That was shit. That was . . . shit. (*Beat.*) Meanwhile, none of this ever happened. Okay?

Ned Yes. . . . Fine. (*They look at each other, smile tentatively. Theo turns away. Ned stares at his back. Fade out.*)

(*In black: the sound of a heavy rain. The rain continues. The light in the apartment is that cocoonish light that comes sometimes on rainy afternoons, a muted array of the colors at the end of the spectrum. There's a fuss at the door. Ned offstage.*)

Ned I'll—

Lina Ooh—I'm shaking it's—

Ned H-here's the key—

Lina Wonderful! (*Key in the lock; they enter, Ned has a grocery bag.*) I'm going to drip all over your nice, dilapidated floor!

Ned Th-that's—me, too.

Lina That was gorgeous, wasn't it?

Ned Yes. . . . G-give me your slicker. (*Lina takes her slicker off and hands it to Ned.*) You're soaked through.

Lina I don't mind. Oh, there aren't any warm fires here, are there? I forget—

Ned No.

Lina Just banked ones (*This is a playful reference to Ned: he doesn't quite catch it.*)—no, nothing.

Ned Y-you're going to catch cold or—

Lina No, I don't. Isn't that moment thrilling, right before it starts, and everything turns purple and the awnings shake and the buildings ignite from the inside? I love that part.

Ned If you . . . n-need to change—

Lina I don't mind just sopping for a while. But is there bourbon?

Ned I . . . No, I don't—

Lina There must be.

Ned S-sorry, I—

Lina I happen to know there is.

Ned ... There is? (*Lina goes to a box on top of a stack of books next to the drafting table and extracts a bottle.*)

Lina Theo is not a big *sharer*.

Ned N-no.

Lina Do you want some? (*Ned waves a hand, "I pass."*) You ought to. It makes everything *so* much better.

Ned Everything's ... fine.

Lina Is it?

Ned ... Today, yes. (*She sips the drink she's poured.*)

Lina Yes. For me, too.
  It was funny running into you.

Ned Yes!

Lina I didn't even realize I was here! I didn't even realize I'd come to this neighborhood. It was not my intention.

Ned What was?

Lina I didn't have one.

Ned M-me, neither.

Lina I was off from the bookstore. I just wandered away the day.

Ned Th-Theo left his robe.

Lina ... Uuuhhh ... well. Segue?

Ned I'm worried about you ... in those things.

Lina You are just desperate to get me out of my clothes, aren't you?

Ned I . . . don't want you to get sick.

Lina . . . Where's the robe?

Ned In the bathroom. On the hook.

Lina I'll change. (*Crosses to bathroom.*) You can change in here when I do. I promise I won't look.

Ned I'm fine.

Lina I promise I won't.

Ned I'm not as wet as you.

Lina No, that's right, I'm *all* wet. Let me bring my drink. (*Passing him.*) I've seen this scene before, you know. (*She goes into the bathroom, keeping the door open a crack. Ned starts unpacking bags onto counter, an array of vegetables, picked for color. Lina calls from bathroom.*) Hey!

Ned What?

Lina Say something small to me while I'm changing!

Ned W-what?

Lina Just chatter at me! I get restless!

Ned I . . . d-don't know what to say.

Lina Just nonsense . . . palaver.

Ned Oh. (*Pause.*) D-do you believe in Original Sin? (*Halfbeat. She pokes her head around the door.*)

Lina (*As though answering his question.*) No, in fact, I don't believe I *have* seen any good movies lately. Why—have *you*?

Ned Oh . . . no. (*Lina emerges in robe.*)

Lina Original Sin!

Ned I—

Lina It's like tea chat with Martin Luther. Why. Do you?

Ned Um, yes, let's change the subject—

Lina No, it's interesting to me—

Ned It's not.

Lina It's just I've grown unaccustomed to the idea—

Ned It's peculiar.

Lina With Theo, there are never any ghosts of any kind. Never any clouds or impediments. He's all sort of sharp and slender and gleaming . . .

Ned . . . He's . . .

Lina . . . Rather a me*tal*lic young man . . .

Ned He's . . . (*Pause.*)

Lina (*Mostly to herself.*) But I swore I wouldn't do that today . . . (*Brightening deliberately.*) What a beautiful harvest on that countertop!

Ned I . . . liked the colors.

Lina Are you going to just leave them there to look at? They'll rot.

Ned No, I—

Lina Or make dinner? I'm not *ang*ling.

Ned . . . I thought I'd m-make dinner. (*Awkward moment.*)

Lina I'll leave when the rain lets up a little.

Ned N-no.

Lina Yes, I will.

Ned Your clothes have to dry.

Lina I can wear them damp.

Ned ... All right. (*He gets a knife, starts chopping vegetables. With sudden gallantry.*) Won't you please stay to dinner?

Lina Give me that knife. (*He yields it. She starts chopping what he was chopping. After a moment, she starts sniffing the air.*) I've always rather *enjoyed* the smell of drenched wool on a person. (*He whips off his sweater. Lights.*)

(*Rain louder. Half-hour later. They're finishing dinner.*)

Lina That was spectacular!

Ned It was ... just a salad.

Lina No. It was like some fall-of-Rome variation on a salad. Every leaf, every herb, every pepper stick.

Ned Th-thank you.

Lina No, thank *you*. ... What time is it, do you know?

Ned The c-clock is broken. Early, though. M-maybe seven? If the rain lets up, we can ... s-see a movie later, if you like.

Lina Yes, we could go out. What's playing?

Ned Mm ... D-down the block, there's *The World of Suzie Wong*.

Lina Or we could stay in.

Ned Either way. Here. (*He pours her the last of the wine, hands it to her, smiles. He's about to say something.*)

Lina What?

Ned Nothing ... I'm ... so happy; it's weird.

Lina (*Puzzled by it.*) Yes! I know, me too!

Ned All day—

Lina Yes, me too! . . . I usually wake in what they call a "brown study." I have no idea what that means but I love to say it—"brown study"—but today . . . I got up and it wasn't raining yet but there was already the scent of it, and I had nothing at all to do. I made some coffee and lit a cigarette and read the dire newspaper and thought, well, all right, yes, give me another sixty years of this.

Ned I—yes—

Lina The two of us waking in a mood like that on the same morning—it's a statistical exorbitance! Given our natures.

Ned Yes—

Lina We have to figure it out: What different thing did our days have in common? (*Pause. They look at each other; a sad recognition neither wants to say aloud.*)

Ned I'll clear the plates. (*He starts to.*)

Lina Let me help you—

Ned No . . . I can.

Lina . . . Okay. (*She sits, lights a cigarette, while Ned cleans off the dishes.*) Has he called you today?

Ned Y-yes.

Lina Oh . . . and how is everything?

Ned He-he's . . . working v-very hard. Apparently, he's had, um, a brainstorm and—

Lina Oh . . . good . . .

Ned Yes . . . he . . . s-says, he's f-finally onto . . . the real thing . . . he n-needed to get away and it's . . . c-come at last. . . . When he comes b-back, we'll have to . . . p-play the March from "Scipio" or s-something . . .
  Hasn't he called you?

Lina Yes. Well, I think so. I'm not sure.

Ned What?

Lina Well, this morning, when I was reading the paper, the phone rang and rang for . . . ten minutes, I think. That was probably him.

Ned Oh. . . . Would you like coffee?

Lina I would dearly love some coffee. (*Ned starts to prepare some.*) Anyway, what did you do today?

Ned It was . . . nothing . . . the same as y-you.

Lina Tell me anyway.

Ned I don't—

Lina I'm getting that feeling—just talk, talk . . . talk it away.

Ned . . . What? Um . . . okay . . . (*They look at each other.*) It was . . . same as you.
    I slept . . . late this morning and when I woke up, it was . . . already raining a little.
    And I felt so . . . light. Free, the way I n-never do. I went to the c-corner to buy coffee and a roll . . . and the pavement was slick and . . . jet in places and the sidewalk was this oily brown in places and . . . there were two women in identical trench coats. One of them h-had just bought an African violet plant and she kept tilting it so dirt kept falling on her . . . feet and . . . it s-surprised her each time so each t-time she would apologize to her . . . shoes, which I liked. I bought the coffee and sipped it and I . . . d-didn't come home right away. I walked out of my way because it was all so . . . pleasant, the day.
    I felt like a . . . flaneur.

Lina What's a flaneur?

Ned Don't you know that word?

Lina No. I don't know that word.

Ned A flaneur is a wanderer through the city. Someone who ... idles through the streets without a purpose ... except to idle through the streets. And linger when it, when it ... pleases him.

Lina That's what he does?

Ned Yes.

Lina What about work? Does he ever get to work?

Ned He has no work ... if he's the real thing.

Lina He just strolls?

Ned Yes. It's his career.
    He has a ... private income.

Lina Some vast sum.

Ned P-pennies but they ... suffice. He d-doesn't need ... much. Not what people need who have ... intricate lives. He just .. walks, you see. His life has no pattern ... just traffic ... and no hope—

Lina That's sad—

Ned Because he has no n-need of hope! The only thing he wants from life is ... the day at hand. And when he's old ... his memories aren't of Triumphs and Tragedies. He remembers ... certain defunct cafes where he shared cups of coffee with ... odd, scary strangers. And people he's known for years and years. Slightly.

Lina Because it's a solitary thing to be a *flaneur*.

Ned Yes ... but never lonely ... I think.

Lina Is that what you want to be?

Ned I haven't g-got the strength of character. But it's what I would w-wish ... for someone better than I am. I think it would be the best thing! To be this . . . vagabond prince. Do you know? A wanderer through the city.

A walker. (*Beat.*)

Lina Tell me about this house you two are making.

Ned No.

Lina Theo never does.

Ned It's . . . idiotic—

Lina It isn't, it's exciting, it makes me want to—

Ned . . . What?

Lina —want to *be* something. I want to be . . . a painter!

Ned You do?

Lina Or . . . a writer, a difficult one!

Ned Oh.

Lina Or a Negro blues singer or just a very intriguing alcoholic. . . . I am so terribly old.

Ned You're young!

Lina I'm a Southern woman who admits to thirty—God alone knows what the truth of things must be!

Ned You're an in-infant.

Lina I'm *nothing*.

Ned You're lovely—

Lina (*On "lovely."*) Theo looks at me and sees . . . something from Anaïs Nin. Just because I'm gloomy, sometimes, and opaque, sometimes. And because when he picked me up, we were sketching naked men at the Art Students League. These sorts of things impress him. He is so naive; he is so easily astonished. He sees me as one of those girls from fifteen years ago: all Quattrocento-pale and dull-eyed and glazed and smugly silent because they possess the secret of the universe and you don't. *I* don't. That's what's funny—I am *never* silent—he must notice that. I smother the day in speech because I know nothing and I want someone to speak back to me and *tell* me—what?

What is it that some people in cities seem to know? What is this secret that is constantly eluding me?

Ned (*Suddenly.*) There isn't any.

Lina . . . What?

Ned There isn't any s-secret. I used to . . . think that, too . . . but, no . . . no secret to be found . . . just . . . g-gestures . . . whims . . . energy . . . personality, do you know?

Lina (*Mordant, but serious.*) That's tragic.

Ned Is it? I thought . . . it was nice . . . when I realized. A relief.

Lina And when was that?

Ned So recently.

Lina Still . . . I want something. . . . I suppose I'll marry Theo and that will be something—

Ned (*Abrupt.*) Is that happening?

Lina Nobody ever says anything, but . . . what else?

I'm so happy for you, that you have this house, that you're beginning something—

Ned I'm not . . . happy about—

Lina But—

Ned It's going to . . . explode in our faces.

Lina No.

Ned We're . . . we *are* too young, m-much too young, no one has . . . ever d-done this so young. We should still be . . . hirelings . . . doing . . . rest rooms and el-elevator shafts, but Theo—

Lina Theo—

Ned He . . . *wants*. No one will ever commission us.

Lina But this *house*—

Ned My p-parents. My parents. No indication at all.

Lina But then you'll have this house and people will see it and come to you.

Ned *I-if* we have it; we're . . . waiting on Theo who's . . . waiting on God who's . . . blocked.

Theo's been a little st-stalled since school and until he gets an idea that's real—

Lina But you said he claims to have one.

Ned . . . Y-yes. He does.

Lina That makes you sad.

Ned No.

Lina It does, though. Why does *he* have to have the idea?

Ned (*Slightly strict.*) Because that's how it is.

Who knows what will come of this anyway? If I minded the prospect of catastrophic failure, I never would have started the whole thing. . . . This is what I imagine will happen: . . . My parents . . . will invest most of the money they have in this h-house . . . as a way of m-making up . . . and the house will never be built . . . or if it is b-built . . . it will collapse due to some mysterious and in-incalculable . . . design flaw. And we will all end up . . . dead. And bankrupt . . . strewn along . . . v-various gutters.

I see this with . . . astonishing clarity.

Bru-brutal clarity. Poverty. Hunger. Aban-bandonment. Incorporated. (*Beat.*) In my ... darkest midnight hours, I ... have this theory that ... (*With one hand, he describes a column.*) Here are ... our intentions ... and here ... (*With the other hand, a parallel column.*) is what actually happens ... and the only thing spanning them (*He connects the two columns on top with an arc.*) is Guilt.

Lina Guilt?

Ned The ... preposterous instinct that we are ... wholly re-responsible for events ... completely out of our control. (*He makes the shapes again.*)
    What we want ... what we get ... guilt: It's an arch.

Lina What you want ... (*She does a line at a fairly low level.*) What you will get ... (*She makes a parallel line at her full reach.*) Genius ... (*A soaring line connecting the two.*) It's a ... Flight Path. An Ascent!

Ned (*Blushes, smiles.*) That's sentimental. ...
    Thank you. (*Beat.*)

Lina You are such a nice man.
    This has been such a wonderful day!
    We have to ... I want to ... If only we really knew *how* to ...

Ned What?

Lina Cherish ... this easy moment ... when we mean so little to each other. (*Pause.*)

Ned I think the coffee's ready.

Lina ... Oh ... oh, yes! (*Ned crosses to the kitchenette.*) I think ... the rain. ... The rain seems to have let up a little. Maybe I should ... skip the coffee and take advantage of—

Ned Your clothes, though ... They may not be ...

Lina Yes, but they may be—

Ned I'll check for you. (*He goes into bathroom, emerges a moment later. A little sadly.*) Oh. They are.

Lina Oh
 . . .
I suppose I really ought to . . .

Ned All right. (*They smile, awkwardly; she crosses to the bathroom, takes her clothes off the curtain rod, and, leaving the door slightly open, starts to change.*) Lina.

Lina (*Pokes head out.*) Yes?

Ned Oh. I just wanted to see . . . if I could . . . say your name . . . without fumbling it.
And I did: L-L-L . . . Lina.

Lina Yes. You did. (*Hesitation. She goes back into bathroom. Ned just stands there. Lina can be glimpsed, shaking dry her clothes. Ned starts to say something. Changes his mind. A moment. He speaks.*)

Ned I'm always w-watching you.
Whenever you're here . . . I can't help it. I try not to. Ev-ever since I met you.
It's awful. . . . I don't want it. . . . I d-don't expect . . . to have things . . . like other people, but I'm . . . always th-thinking of you. It's h-horrible . . .
I kn-know nothing can come of it . . . I know I can't have . . . the things I w-want. I shouldn't tell you this. I ca-can't stop, though. I'm sorry. I'm so sorry.
You're s-so . . . fantastic, you're . . . D-don't let him t-take you down . . . the way he does. Don't let him . . . hurt you. You don't de-deserve it. You deserve only good things. N-not him. Not me. Or . . . I mean, not—(*By now, she has returned to the room. She looks at him.*)

Lina You're just . . . talking on and on—

Ned No.

Lina You are.

Ned I don't waste words. I can't . . . afford to. (*A moment.*) I didn't say anything—

Lina But you did—

Ned F-forget it—

Lina I don't want to. (*The rain is louder now.*) Look—it's started again!
   A downpour. (*Lights.*)

   (*Two days later. The rain continues. Morning. First light. Theo appears in a neutral space—somewhere in the city— thrashing through the rain. He stops as though paralyzed, then moves on. Once he's exited, lights come up in the apartment, revealing Ned and Lina in bed.*)

Lina Was there a moment when you knew how you wanted to spend the rest of your life? Was there a day?

Ned Um, yes, actually. Why?

Lina Tell me.

Ned I was about . . . fifteen. And I wanted to spend the day in the park—Central—the park. I brought a sketch pad because I was afraid somebody might want to talk to me. And—I drew the buildings I was looking up at. Then for no reason I started m-making up my own. And the day was so beautiful, I thought I must be talented. So I kept it up.

Lina What do *I* want?
   You right now in this bed forever.
   I want that.
   And children.

Ned Children?

78

Lina Well . . . one child, at least. One beautiful little girl. Someone precious I can drink with.

Ned I don't like them, much. Ch-children.

Lina . . . No one nice ever says that.

Ned I-I don't feel so bad about it. Plenty of other people l-like them. And most children grow up, so it's not as though I've decided against anyone f-for all time.

Lina How can you not like them, though?

Ned I just . . . n-never know what to say to them. I . . . never was a child . . . much my . . . self and they sc-scare me.

Lina Because they always tell the truth? People say children always tell—

Ned No . . . I don't think they tell the truth. P-people say they tell the truth but . . . those people are stupid. I don't think children are truthful, just . . . terribly candid. Whenever I'm with one I'm afraid it's g-going to point at me and say something humiliating.
Plus, they're boring.
Intensely boring.
And you're constantly being forced to marvel at the tedious things they do. "Johnny counted to five today! F-five!" I don't know what to say to that. I stand there. P-people hate me for that. By the time Johnny gets to t-ten, I'm out of their lives.
But if you want a child, we can have one. (*Beat.*) But you were talking . . . in the abstract, weren't you?

Lina Abstractions are turning into realities very quickly these days. (*They look at each other. Ned wanders over to the drafting table. Lina gets up, puts on robe, tidies the bed a bit or just idles in it. Ned rips a sketch in two. She goes to him, takes the pieces of the sketch from him.*) What are you doing? What is that?

Ned It's nothing—just something I did.

Lina But it's beautiful.

Ned I like to . . . tear them up.

Lina It's remarkable!

Ned Just . . . something I did . . .

Lina How amazing you are. (*While she studies the ripped sketch, Ned takes out a fresh notebook, writes something in it, then closes the book.*) What is *that*?

Ned Nothing.

Lina What *is* that?

Ned (*Shakes his head.*) Nothing.

Lina (*Playful.*) *Tell* me!

Ned It's a journal.

Lina A diary?

Ned No. A journal?

Lina What's the difference?

Ned I'm a boy.

Lina You keep a journal?

Ned Only when I'm happy.

Lina (*Holds out hand.*) Let me.

Ned But—

Lina *Let* me. (*Ned hands it over.*) It's brand-new.

Ned First time I'm happy.

Lina (*Reads.*) "April 3rd to April 5th: Three days of rain." (*She looks up at him.*) That's all?

Ned Sufficient.

Lina But—

Ned I'll know what it means. (*He pulls her toward him.*)

Lina Let me go! I'm going to make breakfast! I'm going to *cook*!

Ned You have that skill?

Lina I've been known to soft-boil an egg in my day. That is, if you have any eggs.

Ned I think there's a couple left over from . . . Christmas or s-something.

Lina Then I'll *hard*-boil them. (*Key in the door. Theo enters.*) Theo. (*Theo looks at her.*)

Ned Theo.
Hi. You weren't supposed to get back till—
Lina's here.
We ran into each other, we s-saw a movie—the rain—she stayed.
You said you were c-coming back tonight. (*Pause.*)

Theo I'm just dropping off my stuff. (*Theo puts down the bag he's carrying, then walks out. Hesitation. Ned starts out after him.*)

Lina Ned?
(*Outside.*)

Ned Theo—

Theo I don't want to talk, Ned.

Ned Theo, listen—

Theo I can't talk yet—

Ned But we—

Theo Just leave me alone—

Ned Look—

Theo I can't—see you—

Ned Theo please . . .

Theo *I didn't bring anything back, okay?* (*Beat.*)

Ned . . . Wh-what?

Theo I don't have anything.
I didn't do the job.

Ned Oh . . . (*A moment. Almost laughing.*) Oh!

Theo I *can't* do this job, Ned. (*Beat.*)

Ned Of course you can.

Theo Don't tell me that anymore!
Don't tell me I can, then explain why I haven't.
Don't—
I keep—
You were right—I've let everybody down—I've hurt everybody.

Ned I never said—

Theo I think I made the wrong choice.
I'm sorry.

Ned Don't apolo— *God*—don't—look—come inside. We'll . . . have breakfast or something—we'll talk—

Theo I can't go in there.

Ned Well what are you going to do?

Theo I don't know.
I'll go someplace.
Washington Square Park or—

Ned In *this*?

Theo . . . someplace. Oh, look, I'll be fine, okay? Just don't tell Lina about any of this. Promise you won't—

Ned But—

Theo Oh, shit. I'm not here, okay? None of this happened, we didn't talk—

Ned Theo—

Theo (*Desperate.*) *How was the movie?*

Ned . . . What?

Theo Please?

Ned . . .
S-so-so. (*A moment.*)

Theo Good. (*Ned looks at Theo. Ned turns back to go into the apartment, then turns back to Theo.*)

Ned Theo?

Theo No—
This will be fine.
Truly. (*Ned returns inside. Theo puts his head up to the rain, soaks in it. Then he stands for a while, uncertain where to go. A moment.*)

Ned Oh, Jesus.

Lina Did you tell him?

Ned (*Amazed; working through the scene that's just happened.*) It didn't . . . come up.

Lina Oh!

Ned That wasn't . . . the t-topic.

Lina How funny.
No.
He seemed too serious to be thinking about me.

Ned He didn't bring anything back.

Lina I didn't imagine he had.

Ned He said he can't . . . do this job.

Lina Well.
There will be other jobs.

Ned God! He's just . . . walking around—

Lina That's all right.

Ned But—

Lina That can be useful.

Ned Oh, man—what I've done!

Lina You have done nothing—

Ned What I've done to him . . . it's like a s-sin—

Lina These puritan categories—they *dom*inate you—

Ned I—

Lina It's fine . . . it's for the best.

Ned What will he d-do?

Lina He's a handsome young man in Manhattan, *something* will happen to him.

Ned B-but—

Lina Oh, this is *Theo*—he will be sad for a minute and then *not* sad. Nothing stops Theo. (*Theo disappears around the corner.*)

Ned I've ruined your life. (*Lina holds him, buries her head in his neck.*)

Lina You've-saved-me-you've-saved-me-you've-saved-me.

Ned (*Softly.*) Oh, I hope so.

Lina I *know*. (*The rain lightens. Lina looks right at Ned.*) Begin.

Ned What?

Lina The house. Begin the house. (*Beat. Ned lets out a nervous laugh.*)

Ned No.

Lina I know you see it. I know you see the whole thing. Don't you?

Ned Yes.
   I know every moment.

Lina Then what are you waiting for?

Ned I don't want to—

Lina *Some*body has to.

Ned I'll . . . *hire* somebody . . .

Lina Neddie—

Ned Things . . . are so much better . . . before they actually start.

Lina Edmund.

Ned Oh. . . . Let's . . . have breakfast . . . d-didn't you say you were going to fix us some—let's go back to bed—

Lina Later. That will be your reward. I'll be your muse!

Ned Oh, Lina.

Lina Oh, *look*—an hour from now I'll cook us a simply wretched breakfast, and we'll sit together and plan what to tell Theo when he gets back, and wallow in remorse, and plot every second of the next two hundred years but *this minute*: turn around. Just draw something. Make a home. (*He turns*

*around, picks up a pencil, finds a fresh sheet of paper. He
makes a first mark.)*

Ned The beginning . . . of error. (*Lina smiles. Ned continues.
Lights fade out.*)

END OF PLAY.